I0621331

Fired to Founder

Exploring Entrepreneurship After Government Service

Merril Gilbert

FoundHer Forward Press™
San Francisco, California

For permissions or inquiries, contact:# FoundHer Forward Press San Francisco, California info@foundherforward.com

Cover and interior design by Asma Younas

Printed in the United States of America

First Edition

ISBN: 979-8-9991153-2-4

FoundHer Forward Press logo used with permission.

Disclaimer

This book is intended for informational and reflective purposes only. It does not constitute legal, financial, or professional business advice. Readers are encouraged to consult with qualified professionals before making decisions related to entrepreneurship, employment, or investments. The author and publisher assume no responsibility for actions taken based on the content of this book.

For Mitchell and Rya, always in my heart filled with love.

Preface: Why Me, Why Now

Let's get one thing straight. I'm not a career coach, a therapist, or some self-proclaimed guru with a morning routine that involves ice baths and enlightenment.

What I am is someone who has worked, quit, been pushed, re-invented, and built again and again. I've lived through market crashes, category launches, startup chaos, and corporate confusion. And for the past 15+ years, I've worked with entrepreneurs across industries to turn shaky ideas into real businesses with actual revenue, real customers, and enough systems in place to avoid complete burnout. I know what it takes to build something stable and profitable, not just shiny. I also know how lonely and terrifying it can feel to start from scratch, especially when the world around you is shifting fast.

This book isn't about glorifying entrepreneurship. It's about exploring whether it's a real path for you, based on who you are, what you care about, and what you're willing to do (and not do).

To help you figure that out, I've included a tool I use often in my work: The Entrepreneurial Readiness Assessment. You'll find the full version inside this book. But it also exists as a standalone resource, something you can return to, share with a friend, or use as a jumping-off point even if you don't read another page.

The *Entrepreneurial Readiness Assessment* isn't here to gate keep the club. It's here to help you figure out if you even want in. If you do, great. If you don't, that's also a powerful move. Either way, this is your moment. Let's find out what's next.

Table of Contents

Fired to Founder

Introduction

Is This… a Business?

Let's be honest. This probably wasn't the plan.

You weren't dreaming of becoming a founder while writing environmental impact statements or managing a federal database. You had a real job, a GS-level paycheck, maybe even a parking space in that brutalist concrete structure you called an office. And then something shifted. The RIF notice.

The "workforce realignment." The dismissal that ignored your specialized expertise and institutional knowledge, whether you'd been there for 2 years or 20 years. The voice in your head that said, "This can't be all there is."

So now you're here, asking what to do next. Maybe you've been sitting with an idea, or maybe just a hunch, and asking the one question no federal training ever covered:

Is this… a business?

This book is for you if you're not sure, but you're ready to find out if this is the time to translate your public service skills into something of your own.

Not "Do I have a business plan?" Not "Will investors understand what I did at Interior?" Just: Is this something I could actually build, run, and make money from using the expertise I've developed?

You have experience. Maybe it's managing grants at EPA. Maybe it's analyzing climate data for NOAA, coordinating emergency responses for FEMA, or developing policy frameworks more complex than most startups can imagine. You've already done hard things. This book will help you translate that into something new.

And yes, this will be messy. Ideas evolve. Markets move. You'll think you've nailed it, and then your spreadsheet will betray you. Like a true frenemy, it will do the math, but not the magic. Don't worry, we'll talk about that too.

What I can tell you is that by the end of this book, you'll know if your idea has legs. You'll know what kind of entrepreneur you are: an Innovator, a Disruptor, a Refiner, or maybe someone ready to take over something already working and make it yours. You'll see how your existing skills, yes, those bureaucratic-sounding bullet points from your federal résumé, can become the foundation of a business that's real, profitable, and deeply yours.

This isn't a step-by-step guide for becoming a millionaire. It's a practical, no-bullshit field manual for figuring out whether your "what if' is worth building, and how to start navigating the private sector without a 200-page standard operating procedure to guide you.

You ready?

Let's go.

Chapter One

The Moment of Change

Is This the End or a New Beginning?

Let's talk about that moment. The one where the job ends, the restructure hits, or you realize that what you've built your life around no longer fits.

Sometimes it's loud, like a formal layoff, a downsizing, or a budget cut. Other times, it's quiet. A growing disinterest. The creeping dread every Sunday night. The feeling that your work, no matter how important on paper, has stopped making sense.

Whether the shift was forced or chosen, something in you changed. And you're not alone. We are living through a massive career redefinition: people leaving (or being pushed out of) long-held roles in government, science, public health, tech, and education. People who've spent years solving complex problems in massive systems are now asking:

What do I do with everything I know, now that no one seems to want it?

That question? It's both terrifying and freeing.

This Wasn't the Plan

You followed the rules. You built experience. You got the clearance. You sat through trainings, performance reviews, inter-agency task forces. And now?

Now you're flipping between job boards and wondering if you're too qualified, too expensive, or just too tired.

Let's pause here.

Because before we get into "what's next," I want you to hear this:

You don't have to have all the answers right now. There is a period of grief. You have to give yourself time and grace. Allow yourself to explore how you feel and what is possible, not just what's probable.

This chapter isn't about rushing to solve the problem. It's about naming where you are and giving you permission to be in it while gently preparing to move through it.

The Emotional Part They Don't Talk About

Let's call it what it is. Losing your job, or stepping away from a path you spent years building, can feel like identity death.

Your job title might not define your whole self, but it did shape how others saw you. Your inbox, your ID badge, your acronyms, gone. Now there's space. And space is loud.

It comes with fear. Guilt. A weird freedom. And a pressure to figure it out fast.

Entrepreneurship, if you choose it, isn't a cure for this feeling. But it can be a container for your skills, your ideas, and your ambition to evolve.

And that's what this book is here to help you explore.

Let's Get Real: What Entrepreneurship Actually Looks Like

This is not a "just manifest it" book. Starting a business is hard. It's confusing. It's also wildly rewarding, for some.

So let's debunk a few myths right out of the gate:

Myth	Reality
You need a groundbreaking idea.	You need a useful idea. Groundbreaking is optional.
Entrepreneurs are fearless.	Most are scared and take action anyway.
You need investors.	Most businesses are self-funded or acquired.
You have to quit your job to start.	You can test things quietly while still employed.
If you build it, they will come.	If you solve a real problem and market it well, some might come.

Entrepreneurship isn't about becoming a founder on the cover of *Fast Company*. It's about building something that makes sense for your life. Something you can own, grow, and run with integrity.

Why Now? (Even If It Feels Like the Worst Time)

Yes, the economy is weird. Yes, AI is rewriting job descriptions faster than HR can post them. Yes, your savings might be feeling the heat.

And still, this might be the best moment to do something new. Why?

Because everything is shifting. And in the cracks of broken systems, new businesses, new models, and new voices emerge.

You don't need to build a tech unicorn. You need to build something useful, needed, and aligned with what you want next.

This book is here to help you figure that out, on your terms.

What's Next: The Readiness Check

You're not expected to have it all figured out today. But you do need to start asking the right questions. That's why we start with the **Entrepreneurial Readiness Assessmen**t.

Not to tell you whether you're cut out for this, but to help you see where you stand and what kind of path (if any) makes sense from here.

The *Entrepreneurial Readiness Assessment* isn't here to gate keep the club. It's here to help you figure out if you even want in.

You'll find it in Appendix A. Let this be the beginning, not the pressure to have an ending.

Chapter Two

Is This a Business?

Understanding Your Entrepreneurial Path

You've got an idea, or maybe just the urge to do something different. But now you're staring at a blank page wondering: Where do I even start?

Not every entrepreneur begins the same way. And not every business needs to be invented from scratch. The startup world might glorify the big, flashy, original idea, but the truth is this: there are multiple ways to build something valuable.

In this chapter, we're breaking it down into four distinct paths. All valid. All real. You don't have to be a visionary genius. What matters is understanding how you think and how you want to work.

The Four Entrepreneurial Archetypes

The Innovator

You see things that don't exist yet and want to bring them into the world. You're inventing a new category, product, or way of solving a problem.

You might be an Innovator if:

- You've been sitting on an idea no one else seems to get, but you know there's something there.

- You create from scratch. New systems. New tech. New food formulas.

- You're okay with ambiguity and risk if it means creating something original.

Example: The iPhone didn't just improve cell phones. It introduced entirely new ways of interacting with technology. There was no swiping, no zooming, no app-based experience before it. It was not a better version of what existed. It changed how we communicate, consume media, and navigate our lives.

The challenge: It takes longer to build. There's no roadmap. You may need more testing, capital, and storytelling upfront.

The Disruptor

You've seen how things work and how they should work. You challenge systems, pricing, delivery models, and power dynamics. You're not reinventing the wheel, but you are making sure it doesn't roll over people.

You might be a Disruptor if:

- You've worked inside a system and know exactly where the friction is.

- You keep thinking, "Why is this still done this way?"

- You want to redesign the structure rather than operate within it.

Example: Lume turned the deodorant category on its head. Not just by changing the ingredients, but by changing where and how it's used. Suddenly, underarm-only became full-body, and legacy brands had to scramble to keep up.

The challenge: Disruption takes clarity and stamina. You're not just changing how something works; you're challenging why it exists in the first place. That means you'll need a strong case, a solid model, and the ability to lead others through discomfort.

The Refiner

You don't want to reinvent the wheel; you want to make the wheel better. You improve processes, experiences, and offerings that already work, just not well.

You might be a Refiner if:

- You're obsessed with fixing things, improving systems, and simplifying the complex.

- You find inefficiencies and can't stop yourself from stream-lining them.

- Your steady, analytical, and patient but still driven.

Example: Look at the evolution of dog food. The category's been around forever, but now there's fresh food, refrigerated food, subscription delivery, and ingredient transparency that didn't exist ten years ago. Same product. Way better experience.

The challenge: Refiners don't always get the spotlight. But they do get results. Success here comes from quiet excellence, not loud launches.

The Acquirer

You don't want to start from scratch; you want a head start. You're buying an existing business and making it better, stronger, or more aligned with your values.

You might be an Acquirer if:

- You love digging into operations and seeing what's already working.

- You'd rather scale something existing than build something new.

- You're not afraid to negotiate, restructure, or evolve an inherited model.

Example: Accounting firms, plumbing businesses, dry cleaners, are staples of every community. Many of them are owned by people looking to retire. Smart entrepreneurs are stepping in, modernizing operations, and keeping the business going.

The challenge: Acquiring isn't just about writing a check. It requires due diligence, leadership, and knowing what not to change.

So... Which One Are You?

You might already know, or you might be a mix. That's okay.

This isn't a personality quiz. It's a way to start thinking more clearly about the path ahead. Your entrepreneurial type can guide how you build, what kind of support you need, and how to talk about your business when you're ready to go public.

Try this quick check-in:

- What excites you more: creating, fixing, shaking up, or taking over?

- Do you feel more energized by a blank canvas or by refining something real?

- Are you more risk-tolerant or stability-seeking?

- Do you want freedom, impact, efficiency, or legacy?

Your answers won't lock you into a box. But they'll help you design a business that actually fits you, not just a mold.

Why This Matters

Too many people burn out trying to be the wrong kind of entrepreneur. Innovators think they have to disrupt. Refiners feel pressure to start from scratch. Acquirers are treated like they "cheated" because they bought into something proven.

Here's the truth: your model is valid. Your mindset is an asset. Your background is your edge.

What matters most is not how you start. It's that you start in a way that works for you.

Next up, we'll talk about how to take that spark of an idea or the bones of an existing business and see if it has real traction. Because before you raise money, build a brand, or quit your job, you've got to answer one simple question:

Does this solve a problem people care enough to pay for?

Let's find out.

Chapter Three

Finding the Spark

From Idea to Validation

L et's cut to it: not every idea is a business.

Some are hobbies. Some are wild thoughts scribbled in the margins of a notebook. Some are late-night texts to your smartest friend that you immediately regret in the morning.

But some ideas? They stick. They wake you up. They start connecting dots between your past experience and what people actually need right now.

This chapter is about figuring out which is which.

What Makes an Idea Worth Pursuing?

The big myth is that businesses start with inspiration. What they really start with is observation.

You noticed something broken. Something inefficient. Something wildly inconvenient. Or something that should exist, but doesn't.

A spark happens when you connect that observation with something you're uniquely positioned to solve.

So ask yourself:

- What frustrates me that others just seem to accept?

- What do people always ask me for help with?

- What do I already know how to do that others would pay for?

You don't need a moonshot. You need a real problem and a credible path to solve it.

Passion Project or Business?

Not everything you love is meant to be monetized. And not everything you hate doing is unmarketable.

Here's a quick check:

If it's a passion project...	If it's a business idea...
You'd do it even if no one paid you.	You want to know if people will pay you.
It's creative or expressive for its own sake.	It's built to solve a specific need.
It doesn't need a roadmap.	It benefits from systems and structure.
You're fine keeping it small.	You see potential for revenue or scale.

Some passion projects evolve into businesses. Some shouldn't. This book is here to help you make that call before you burn out trying to commercialize joy.

Ways to Find Your Spark

Depending on your archetype, the idea might come from different angles:

Innovators look for missing tools, services, or systems. What doesn't exist yet that should?

Disruptors look at what's outdated. What's overpriced, unfair, or inefficient?

Refiners look at what's already working. What can you make better, simpler, smarter?

Acquirers look at businesses already running. What's for sale? Who's retiring? Where is there value that just needs better leadership?

You don't have to invent something to be an entrepreneur. You just have to spot opportunity and know how to test it.

Let's Talk About Testing

This is the part most people skip and regret later.

Testing doesn't mean launching a full website, filing an LLC, or ordering branded shipping boxes. It means talking to people. Asking real questions. Putting a prototype or offer in front of someone and watching what happens.

Try:

- A short survey to your network

- A pop-up at a local event

- A "beta" offer on social media

- A service offered to three people at a discount, in exchange for feedback

- Calling a business owner and asking if they're looking to sell

What you're looking for is evidence. Proof that someone other than you want this and will pay for it.

What If You're Selling a Service?

You don't need a product to be a business owner. Some of the most successful businesses are built around services—deep expertise, specialized knowledge, or the ability to solve problems no one else wants to touch.

If you're considering consulting, freelancing, or contract work, that is entrepreneurship. You're still building something of your own.

Consultants often operate under the radar, but they're making decisions every day about pricing, clients, scope, capacity, and impact. That's not side work. That's a business.

Here's what matters:

- What do you know that others don't?

- Who needs it badly enough to pay for it?

- How do you want to work, and for how long?

Maybe you help government agencies modernize. Maybe you help startups navigate policy. Maybe you design training programs or synthesize data for funders. These are real services, and they scale in different ways than physical products.

Your "spark" might come from a process you've used successfully in your past job, or something people keep asking you to do again. It's valid. It's needed. And it belongs in the entrepreneurship conversation.

And If You're Buying Instead of Building

Sometimes the idea isn't yours. It's someone else's, and they're done with it. They want to retire, move on, or just need someone who can take it further.

There's value in buying something with:

- Existing customers

- Cash flow

- Brand equity

- Systems that work (even if they're outdated)

The spark, in that case, is about recognizing potential, not invention. That still counts.

What to Watch Out For

A good idea doesn't mean good timing. And even the best idea can fall flat if:

- No one's willing to pay for it

- You're solving a problem that doesn't actually exist

- It requires resources you don't have (yet)

- You can't clearly explain what it does and who it's for

Before you spend time, money, or emotional bandwidth, stress test the idea. Try saying it out loud to someone who isn't your friend.

If they say, "Oh, that's interesting," and change the subject, keep refining.

If they say, "Wait, I need that," you might be onto something.

Before You Move On: Is This Worth Testing?

You don't need to write a business plan or build a prototype. But you do need to pause and ask:

Is this idea real, or just interesting?

Say your answers out loud to these five questions:

1. Who is this for? Be specific.

2. What problem does it solve?

3. How is the problem currently being addressed?

4. Why are you the person to solve it?

5. What would you offer first, just to see if anyone responds?

If you can't answer all five, that's okay. But don't ignore them. These questions are your first test. They help you figure out if your idea is worth pursuing or if it needs more thinking before you move forward.

What Comes Next

You've got the spark. Maybe even more than one.

Now the real question is: Who else cares about this, and will they actually pay for it?

In the next chapter, we'll talk about **market fit**. You'll learn how to figure out who your idea serves, what they truly need, and how to stop guessing and start connecting.

A good idea is only half of the equation. The other half is the person who needs it.

Chapter Four

Market Fit

Finding Your Niche and Audience

L et's say your idea has some legs. Now comes the part that trips people up: figuring out who else actually wants it.

Because a business doesn't exist in a vacuum. It exists when someone else says, "Yeah, I need that, and I'm willing to pay for it."

This chapter is about that person. Or group of people. Or organization. Who they are, how they think, and how to stop talking to the wrong ones.

The Difference Between a Cool Idea and a Real Business

A cool idea is something people nod at. A real business is something people commit to.

Your job now is to stop making assumptions and start listening. Not to everyone. Just to the people who matter.

So ask:

- Who is already trying to solve this problem?

- What are they doing now that isn't working?

- What are they saying, buying, or avoiding that gives you clues?

You're not trying to find customers. You're trying to understand humans. What motivates them, what frustrates them, and what moves them to act.

You're Not for Everyone, and That's the Point

Trying to appeal to everyone is the fastest way to connect with no one. A strong market fit starts with focus.

That might look like:

- Parents of children with food sensitivities, not all parents

- Small-town health clinics with limited staff, not just healthcare

- Independent contractors filing quarterly taxes, not everyone who needs accounting

- Mid-career women in transition, not anyone on LinkedIn

Focus doesn't mean forever. It just means starting somewhere real.

Testing Fit Without Fancy Tools

You don't need a market research firm. You need curiosity and a search bar.

Start with:

- Trade association websites and industry newsletters

- Recent news stories about your category or audience

- Google search trends and forums (yes, Reddit counts)

- Browsing retailer shelves or online listings to see pricing, packaging, and how the competition is positioned

If you're building a product, look at where and how it's sold. Pricing tells you where you can compete. People will pay more for something they perceive is better, solves a deeper need, or hits the market first.

The most expensive time for a product is usually at launch, before you scale, before you gain production efficiency. Differentiation is your edge in the early stage. Being clear on how your offering stands out is what makes a business sustainable, not just exciting.

Also try this:

- Ask three to five people you trust: Would this solve a problem you actually have?

- Post a version of your idea on social media and watch who comments, shares, or saves it

- Use Instagram, TikTok, or YouTube to test positioning. Many people under 40 get their news, product inspiration, and life advice from these platforms. They are not just for entertainment. They are modern research tools

- Email your old network, but only the ones who understand what you're trying to do

- Go where your potential audience already gathers. Slack groups, LinkedIn threads, conferences, or coworking events

You're not looking for praise. You're looking for resonance. That moment where someone says, "Wait. I actually need this".

You're Not Just Selling a Thing. You're Building Trust

People don't just buy products or services. They buy with emotion. They buy because they believe it will solve something they care about. They buy stories that feel true to their needs.

This is where a lot of smart people fall into the explaining trap. They spend so much time proving their expertise that they forget the audience is asking one thing:

Can you help me?

That means:

- Your message has to be clear, not clever
- Your offer has to be obvious, not overdesigned
- Your relevance has to be felt, not explained

Don't lead with your resume. Lead with their problem. Then show how your experience helps solve it.

If You're Offering a Service, This Still Applies

Service-based entrepreneurs sometimes skip this step because they assume, "I am the market."

But even if you're consulting, you still need to define your audience and how your service meets their needs right now.

For example:

- Are you helping government agencies or nonprofits navigate policy shifts or new mandates after restructuring?

- Are you guiding early-stage founders through regulatory or compliance challenges?

- Are you serving impact investors who need operational due diligence?

Each audience speaks differently, thinks differently, and buys differently.

Your service won't land unless you meet them where they are. Use their language, their goals, and their urgency.

Why Market Fit Isn't One and Done

Your idea might evolve. Your audience might surprise you. That's not failure. That's adaptation.

You'll test a message that doesn't land. You'll talk to someone who seems perfect and they'll ghost you. You'll think you found your niche, and then it shifts.

Good. That's part of building something alive. Something responsive. Something real.

Before You Move On

Ask yourself:

- Who am I building this for?

- Why them?

- Where do they already spend time and money?

- How can I reach them now, not six months from now?

Your audience is out there. Find them. Talk to them. Listen.

And when they say, "This is what I need," pay attention.

What Comes Next

Now that you know who you're building for, it's time to talk about you.

In the next chapter, we flip the lens and ask a different question:

Why you, and why now?

Because a business needs two things to stand: A market that wants it, and a founder who's ready to lead it.

Let's figure out if that's you.

Chapter Five

Why You, Why Now?

Your Advantage Is Already in the Room

Here's the moment where most people flinch.

They have an idea. They have done some testing. Maybe they have even talked to potential customers.

And then the doubt creeps in.

Who am I to do this? I've never built a business before. There are already people doing this better. I'm not qualified enough.

This chapter is here to cut through that noise and ask a better question:

Why are you the right person to do this, right now?

Because if your idea has traction, the next variable is you.

You're Not Starting from Zero

You have experience. It might not come with startup buzzwords or tech credentials, but it's real and transferable.

Maybe you have:

- Managed crisis response across multiple agencies

- Run cross-functional teams in high-pressure environments

- Written policy that changed lives

- Built training programs that actually worked

- Navigated bureaucracy without losing your mind

- Worked across manufacturing or regulatory compliance systems

These are not soft skills. These are leadership, operations, systems, and execution skills.

You have already solved harder problems than most founders deal with in year one. Now it's about repurposing that experience in a new context.

What matters most right now is not having every answer. It's the willingness to try, to ask better questions, to make mistakes, and try again. That mindset is more valuable than any credential.

Own the Gap You See

Most businesses start because someone saw something missing.

That gap you noticed, the inefficiency you can't ignore, or the group no one is serving. That's not just insight. That's your origin story.

You are not building this business despite your background. You are building it because of it.

So ask yourself:

- What have I seen that others missed?

- What pain point keeps showing up in every job I've had?

- What do people come to me for, over and over again?

This is your edge. This is where experience becomes leverage.

Stop Waiting for Permission

No one is going to tap you on the shoulder and say, "You're ready now."

There is no certification for being a founder. No final exam. No clearance level.

You can be deeply experienced and still feel like an outsider. That doesn't mean you're unqualified. It means you're stepping into something new.

You don't need to feel fearless. You just need to feel willing.

Willing to test. Willing to ask for feedback. Willing to build as you go.

But What If I Still Feel Like an Imposter?

That's not a flaw. It's part of the process. You're doing something new, high-stakes, and personally meaningful. Of course you feel the weight of it.

Try this:

- That's not a flaw. It's part of the process. It means you're human.

- Remember that confidence is built by doing, not waiting

- Accept that no one feels fully ready, and still, they begin

Imposter syndrome is loudest when you have outgrown the old version of yourself but have not fully stepped into the new one.

This chapter is the bridge.

Don't Compete. Differentiate.

Someone else is already doing it? Good. That means there's demand. But no one else can bring your specific lens, your background, and your approach.

You don't have to be the best. You have to be relevant and believable to the people you are here to help.

That might look like:

- Being the translator between two worlds you've worked in

- Bringing transparency to an industry that runs on secrecy

- Adding systems thinking to a creative field

- Bringing humanity to a data-driven model

You are not just another voice. You are a voice from experience.

You Can Also Collaborate

Not everything needs to be built alone. Sometimes the smartest move is to partner, license, or co-create.

Look for:

- Adjacent businesses with similar customers

- Products that could be stronger with your approach layered in

- Services that need better implementation, education, or storytelling

- Founders who need an operator, not another idea

Your value might not be starting something solo. It might be expanding or refining something already in motion.

Before You Move On

Ask yourself:

- What do I know deeply that others overlook?

- What have I done in past roles that applies directly here?

- Why am I the person to do this now?

- Who would be better off because I stepped up?

You don't have to prove your worth. You just have to recognize it, and start using it to build what's next.

Chapter Six

How It Makes Money

Because a Business Without Revenue Is Just a Project

At some point, your idea needs to pay for itself. That does not mean it has to be profitable in month one, but it does mean you need a plan for how it supports you and sustains itself.

But first, let's define what we mean by a business. A business is not just something you love doing. It's not a logo, a website, or a clever name. A business is a system that delivers value in exchange for money. Whether you're selling products, services, software, expertise, or licensing intellectual property, what matters is that there is an exchange: something you offer, something someone else wants, and a clear way to get paid. Defining your business model early helps you figure out what you're really building. Is it a side hustle? A full-time company? A consulting practice? A consumer product brand? There's no wrong answer. But clarity here is what separates an idea from a functioning business.

This chapter is about how money actually moves through a business. Ideas are free. Execution costs money. Growth costs even more.

So let's talk about how this thing earns. Not in theory, but in reality.

Know Your Revenue Model

A business model is just a way of answering the question, **"How does this make money?"**

Here are a few common types:

Product-Based

You sell a physical or digital item. Think food, skincare, books, or an app.

Service-Based

You sell your time, expertise, or a result. Think consulting, coaching, design, or audits.

Subscription or Membership Recurring revenue, usually monthly or annually. Think a newsletter, meal kit, or learning platform.

Licensing or IP-Based You create something that others pay to use. Think patented tech, curriculum, or white-label formulations.

Marketplace or Platform You make money when others make money. Think Airbnb, Etsy, or a specialized B2B exchange.

You don't need to memorize every model. You need to know which one fits what you are building and how your customer prefers to buy.

Pricing Is a Strategy and a Math Problem

Pricing is not about guessing or undercutting the competition. It is a combination of logic, research, and value positioning.

Start with research. What are others charging for something similar? Not just what's listed online. Look at what actually sells, and where.

Then work backward. What does it cost to produce or deliver your product or service? What do you need to cover monthly expenses, including your time? How much can your intended customer afford, and what will they accept?

With products, founders often forget to include their own pay. They say, *"I'll skip a salary until I scale,"* but that mindset usually builds an unsustainable model. Your compensation must be part of the price, even if you defer collecting it early on.

Services work differently. You are selling expertise, results, or access. That means the perceived value will vary. Even if you start small, your pricing should reflect the transformation or clarity you deliver, not just the hours you spend doing the work.

Revenue Does Not Equal Profit

A thousand-dollar sale is not a thousand dollars in your pocket.

There are costs:

- Materials and inventory
- Labor (even if it's just you)
- Marketing, shipping, software, bookkeeping

- Taxes, transaction fees, and unexpected expenses

Profit is what's left after those costs are paid. Loss is when you bring in less than it takes to operate.

In the early stages, you might operate at a loss for a while, especially as you test, improve, and build awareness. That doesn't mean you're failing. It means you're learning. But the goal is to move toward profitability as quickly and sustainably as possible.

Knowing the difference between revenue, expenses, and profit helps you make smarter decisions about pricing, capacity, and what to say yes to. You don't need perfect spreadsheets. You need visibility: where money comes in, where it goes, and how long you can sustain the current pace.

Profitability is not about getting rich fast. It's about building something that lasts. That means reaching a point where the business supports itself, supports you, and allows for growth without constant financial strain.

That's where early-stage stability comes in.

What Early Stability Looks Like

In the first year, your goal is not growth at all costs. It's stability.

Can this business generate enough money to cover its costs, support your time, and show signs of life?

That might look like:

- Starting with a consulting offer while your product line develops

- Taking on short-term work that funds your early stage

- Testing services before investing in systems

- Pricing smartly so that each sale helps move you forward

Stability is what allows you to keep going while you figure things out. It is your on-ramp to profitability, not a detour.

If you are building something tied to climate, local production, or resource efficiency, then sustainability might be part of your impact model too. But regardless of industry, what stability looks like will depend on how your business earns.

If you're offering a service, it may take time to build trust, attract the right clients, and reach consistent demand. If you're creating a product, it often takes even longer. Getting to market fit, securing trial, and earning repeat purchases are all part of the growth curve.

Early stability is not a straight line. It is about building momentum, understanding your business model, and having a clear sense of what needs to happen next.

About That Passive Income Myth

Once you have a clearer picture of how your business earns and what stability looks like, it's easy to start looking for shortcuts. One of the most common traps is the idea that you can skip the work by building "passive income."

Let's talk about what that really means. And what it takes to get there.

You've heard it: make money while you sleep. And yes, some business models can support that. But not from day one.

Passive income is usually built from a highly active foundation. The product, course, platform, or system has to be developed, tested, marketed, and maintained.

So do not start with "set it and forget it." Start with "test it and make it better." If it works, you can build systems that make it more scalable over time.

Before You Move On

Ask yourself:

- How does this business actually make money?

- What does it cost to run, realistically?

- What do I need to earn in the next six months to keep going?

- What would I need to charge to make that possible?

You do not have to be a financial expert. But if this is going to be a business, money has to be part of the plan.

It is not just about making sales. It is about building something that supports your work and your life.

What Comes Next

Now that you know how money comes in and what it takes to keep things going, it is time to talk about getting legitimate.

In the next chapter, we get into the operational foundation: what to file, what to protect, and when to ask for help.

Because building a real business means setting it up to succeed.

Chapter Seven

Getting Legit

Setting Up Your Business to Survive (Not Just Launch) The Boring but Necessary Stuff

Let's pause for a moment before we get into the details.

I'm not a lawyer or an accountant. This chapter is not legal advice. It is here to help you understand what is typically required to set up a functioning business, so you know what questions to ask, what steps to research, and where to begin.

There are plenty of free and low-cost resources out there: your state's registration portal, blogs from sites like GoDaddy or Stripe, the IRS and SBA websites (when they are working), and tools like ChatGPT. The point is not to master every detail. It's to take action and understand what you're stepping into.

If you are reading this book, chances are your former system has been dismantled. Government roles, scientific institutions, and regulatory agencies have been disbanded or defunded. And now, here you are, stepping into something new. You are not building a business for the IRS or your LinkedIn profile. You are doing it to protect your time, money, and energy, so you can keep going.

Think of this chapter as a practical setup guide. Just enough structure to move forward without breaking under the weight of it.

Don't Over-Structure on Day One

You don't need to rush into forming a company the minute your idea takes shape. But once money starts moving, you need some guardrails.

The goal is to stay lean while reducing personal risk. Just enough structure to operate responsibly and grow when the time is right.

So, what is a business structure, and why does it matter?

A business structure is the legal framework that defines how your business operates. It impacts how you are taxed, how you get paid, how you are held liable if something goes wrong, and how your business grows in the future.

Are you the business, or is it something separate from you? Can you bring on partners? Raise money? Deduct expenses?

You do not need to know all the answers now. But the structure you choose sets the tone for how you will operate and can save you from major complications later.

Start with a Business Name

You can change it later, but you do need something to operate under.

Start by making sure the name is available:

- Can you get the .com or a relevant domain?

- Is the name already in use in your state or county?

- Is there an active trademark filed with that name?

- Are there similar businesses that would confuse a customer?

A unique name makes it easier to claim your digital space. But don't get stuck. You can rebrand later if needed. Just avoid choosing something too close to an existing business in your category, or you risk legal issues and SEO chaos.

Choose a Business Structure That Fits

A business structure is the legal and financial framework that defines how your business operates. It determines how you're taxed, how you get paid, how you're protected, and how you can grow.

Here's what most early-stage founders need to know:

Sole Proprietor You are the business. Easiest setup and lowest cost. But there is no separation between your personal and business liability.

LLC (Limited Liability Company) Offers liability protection and flexibility. Works well for solo founders or partnerships. Common for consulting, product sales, and creative businesses.

S-Corp or C-Corp More complex. Often used by businesses planning to raise money or issue stock. If that is not your plan right now, you can wait.

Choosing a structure depends on your goals, risk tolerance, and long-term plans. Many first-time founders start with something simple and adjust as their business evolves. It's worth reviewing the options, then seeking advice from a legal or tax professional before making a decision.

Open a Business Bank Account

This is not about being fancy. It is about being clear. Separate your business and personal funds.

Even if you are only bringing in a few hundred dollars, this sets the tone for how you treat your business. You do not need a business credit card right away. But you do need a clean way to track income and expenses from day one.

Contracts, Insurance, and Other Grown-Up Moves

If you're offering services or working with others, you need contracts. Even a simple one-page agreement can save you from confusion or disputes later.

Look into:

- Client contracts

- Contractor agreements

- Non-disclosure agreements (NDAs)

- Licensing or distribution terms

- Terms of service and privacy policies for websites or apps

Also consider business insurance, especially if you sell physical products, give professional advice, work on-site, or handle client data.

Common types include:

- General liability

- Professional liability (errors and omissions)

- Product liability

- Cyber insurance

Talk to a small business insurance broker. You might not need much right away, but knowing what exists gives you a better sense of what to budget for and when to add protection.

Contracts Are Not Optional

Let's stay on this point a little longer, because it is that important.

Even if it's your friend. Even if it's a handshake deal. Even if they say, "We'll figure it out later."

You need a contract.

At minimum, it should include:

- What you are delivering

- When and how it will be delivered

- Payment terms

- What happens if someone backs out, doesn't pay, or changes the scope

- Confidentiality and information protection

- Clear rights to any original work, content, or systems you create

Start with a solid template or talk to a lawyer. You do not have to be litigious. You do have to be protected.

Protect What You're Building

Your work has value. Treat it that way.

Start with the basics:

- Make sure your business name is available

- Lock down your domain and social handles

- Add copyright or usage language to anything original

- Save copies of your formulas, content, and documentation somewhere secure

If you are developing something proprietary whether it is a product formula, a training method, or a research model keep a clear record of your development. It doesn't have to be formal or filed in a government database, but it should be time-stamped and stored.

In today's world, a digital paper trail is just as important as physical documentation.

You can use tools like:

- Google Drive or Dropbox for file storage and date tracking

- Zoom or Descript to record demonstrations or tutorials

- Canva, Figma, or Miro to map out visual and brand concepts

- HelloSign or DocuSign to lock down contracts or NDAs

You don't need to be overly precious about early-stage work. But you should be able to show what you've built, and when you built it, if anyone ever asks.

Digital Hygiene and Online Setup

Once your name and structure are in place, set up your digital foundation.

At minimum:

- Register your domain

- Create a basic website or landing page

- Set up a business email

- Reserve your social media handles, even if you're not using them yet

- Store your business documents in one organized, secure place

Digital clutter slows everything down. Starting with simple systems makes your life easier when the pace picks up.

Know When to Bring in Experts

You do not need to hire a full team. You do need to know when to stop guessing.

Start here:

- Schedule one conversation with an accountant or CPA

- Find a business attorney to review your contracts or company setup

- Explore tools like Gusto, Wave, QuickBooks, Stripe, LegalZoom, or HelloSign

There are also nonprofit programs and Small Business Development Centers that offer free or low-cost legal and financial help. Many are funded by local governments, universities, or grant programs.

Getting expert advice early does not mean you are doing something wrong. It means you are investing in doing it right.

Trusted Advisors Are Not a Shortcut

Everyone talks about "finding a mentor." That is not a job title. It is a relationship built on respect, shared values, and aligned timing.

Great advisors are out there, but they are not waiting to do free consulting in your DMs.

Instead of hunting for someone to fix everything, focus on building real relationships with people who are invested in your growth.

Start with your network. Reach out to someone who understands your field. Ask specific questions. Be open to feedback. Follow up with a thank you, not a pitch.

When someone offers their time, show up prepared. When someone shares their experience, listen before you react. When someone gives you their brainpower, respect it—even if they are not invoicing you yet.

Not all advisors will expect compensation, but many will. That might mean a paid session, a retainer, a formal advisory agreement, or equity in your business. If someone brings consistent value, do not expect it to stay casual forever.

The right advisor does not give you a roadmap. They help you build your own with fewer wrong turns.

Start Lean. Stay Focused. Build What Matters.

This chapter is not here to overwhelm you. It is here to help you build a foundation that supports your work without slowing it down.

Getting legit does not mean spending thousands before you are ready. It means putting enough structure in place to protect your time, energy, and future decisions.

You can start lean. Plenty of businesses begin with a setup that is strong enough to grow and light enough to evolve.

If you are not ready to file anything yet, that is okay. Use this chapter as a checklist. Start where you are. Add what you need when you need it.

Just make sure you are protected enough to move forward with confidence.

The real risk is ignoring this entirely, then rushing through it later under pressure. That is when mistakes happen.

Before You Move On

Ask yourself:

- Have I picked the right structure for now?

- Is my money cleanly separated?

- Do I have at least one contract I understand and can reuse?

- Am I protecting the most important things I'm building?

- Do I know where to find trusted legal and financial advice if I need it?

- Have I started a list of potential mentors, advisors, or experts I can learn from?

You do not need a fancy setup to look official. You need clarity, coverage, and enough order to support what is next.

What Comes Next

Structure is one thing. Getting someone to care is another.

In the next chapter, we'll get into brand, message, and how to talk about what you do in a way that actually connects. Because a business that works on paper still needs people to believe in it.

Chapter Eight

Make Them Care

The Brand Begins Before the Business

Most people don't remember the exact moment they had a great business idea. They remember the moment someone believed in it, or at least understood what they were trying to do.

That is what a brand does. It tells the story of your idea before it is even real.

This chapter is not about logos or color palettes. It is about building something people connect to because it feels human, purposeful, and possible.

That work starts now. Not once the business is launched, but while you are still figuring it out.

Your Brand Is a Blend of Head and Heart

You are not just building a business. You are creating an experience, a voice, a way of showing up in the world.

That takes logic and strategy. It also takes instinct.

What do you want this business to feel like? What do you want to be known for? What do you want people to remember after five seconds, or five minutes?

It is not about having all the answers. It is about staying curious and capturing what moves you.

Start a Brand Scrapbook

This is your modern mood board. But it is not just about visuals.

It is anything that helps define your business's vibe, values, or voice. Start collecting:

- Notes on what inspires you

- Photos of competitor packaging or store displays

- Audio clips or podcast quotes that stick with you

- Headlines that caught your attention

- Product pages you wish you wrote

- Your own voice memos or late-night ideas

You are building a living story of what this thing could be and why it matters.

Not just for your audience. For you.

Show What You're Building, Even Before It's Built

People don't just buy products. They buy belief.

You don't need a brand guide or a perfect pitch. But you do need to start showing what your idea looks and feels like.

That might mean:

- A short video explaining your concept

- A prototype sketch or mock-up

- A photo of something that inspired your offering

- A few sentences describing the problem you want to solve

These glimpses make it real. They help others see the potential, and they help you spot what resonates.

Show Up on Video, Even If You Hate It

If you didn't grow up filming yourself on a phone, video might feel like a stretch. But it matters. People trust people, especially when it comes to services, consulting, or early-stage brands.

You do not have to go viral or look polished. You just need to get comfortable showing up.

A great place to start is <u>Kendra Losee's 14-Day Camera Confidence Challenge</u>.
It is designed for people who want to learn how to be themselves on camera without overthinking it.

Practice builds comfort. Comfort builds confidence. And confidence builds connection.

Use AI to Spark Ideas, Not Define Them

AI tools like ChatGPT, Claude, Midjourney, DALL·E, and Canva's AI generator can help you brainstorm and test concepts quickly.

Use prompts like:

- "Describe three types of customers who might want this."

- "What language would appeal to a values-driven audience in their 40s?"

- "Write a tagline for a brand that is bold, practical, and a little rebellious."

- "Create sample imagery for a modern take on vintage design."

AI will not tell you who you are. But it can help you explore who you might be. You still choose the direction. AI just gives you options to respond to.

Step Into the Future You Want to Build

Every brand starts with a hunch. A scribble. A passing thought that lingers longer than expected.

You do not need a polished plan to act like a founder. You just need to pay attention.

Start by noticing what excites you. Capture the ideas that show up when you are not trying so hard. Save the photos, headlines, quotes, and voice memos that feel like something you might create or become.

You are building belief. First in yourself, and eventually in others. And that begins by staying curious about the kind of business you want to build and who you want it to connect with.

Before You Move On

Ask yourself:

- What inspires the brand I want to create?

- How am I capturing the essence of this business before it exists?

- Where can I start showing up visually or verbally, even in a small way?

- What part of this idea could I test or share right now?

- Am I using tools like AI and video to explore, not replace, my creativity?

A strong brand does not start with a mission statement. It starts with paying attention to the details.

Start there. The rest will follow.

Because once you begin to show up, people will start paying attention too.

And that brings us to what comes next: the people around you. The ones who will shape, challenge, and strengthen the business you're building.

Chapter Nine

Who's Around You Matters

Support, Skills, Sanity, and the Stuff You Can't Learn Alone

Entrepreneurship can look like a solo path. But if you try to do everything alone, you will burn out before the business even takes off.

You need support. You need help building what you do not know yet. And you need people around you who keep you grounded, not just impressed.

This chapter is about the ecosystem around your business. The people you hire. The ones you learn from. The ones who talk you out of quitting on the wrong day.

If the last few chapters were about what you are building, this one is about who helps make it possible.

Learn What You Don't Know (Yet)

Let's start with a reality check. You are not expected to know everything. But you are expected to learn.

Before you hire someone or outsource a task, ask yourself: Is this something I can reasonably learn? Or is it better to pay someone who already knows?

For the first category, there is no shortage of options. Online courses, community colleges, bootcamps, and even YouTube can help you build business literacy and confidence without draining your budget.

Look into:

- LinkedIn Learning (great for marketing, productivity, and operations)

- Coursera or edX (industry-specific, university-taught)

- General Assembly (tech and product-focused)

- Teachable or Skillshare (real-world creatives sharing real-world lessons)

- Your public library (you would be surprised what is free with a card)

Some fields require certifications to build trust or meet legal standards. If you are entering a regulated industry or a role that relies on expertise, such as coaching, HR, or wellness, earning the right credentials can strengthen your business and increase your authority.

This is not about stacking certificates just to feel legitimate. It is about learning what you need so you can deliver with confidence and make better decisions as you grow.

Hire for Where You're Going

At some point, you will need help.

That might look like a part-time assistant, a contractor, or a co-founder.

It could be someone who builds your website or someone who builds out your team.

Early hires matter more than people think. They are not just filling a role. They are helping shape the company.

Hire for skills you do not have. Hire people who can work without needing you to micromanage every detail. Hire people who know how to build, not just maintain. You do not need a resume full of big names. You need someone who can show up, follow through, and think beyond the job description.

Build in Your Community

You do not have to go far to find people who can help you grow. But you do have to show up.

Look around:

- Local coworking spaces

- Small business workshops

- Grant programs and incubators

- Chamber of Commerce events

- Maker collectives, food labs, or artist hubs

- Business associations tied to your industry or identity

Relationships are built over time. The people who connect you to new opportunities tomorrow are often the ones you showed up for today.

Two People You Need in Your Corner

This part is not about strategy. It is about staying sane.

There are two kinds of support you need as a founder, and neither requires a formal pitch.

1. The No-Matter-What Person This is someone who loves you regardless of how the business is going. They might not understand what you are building, but they are always glad to hear from you. Call them when everything feels like too much. Let them remind you who you are.

2. The Constructive Truth Teller This person is honest but kind. They will not coddle you, but they will not destroy you either. They will say, "You are going in circles" or "You are avoiding the real issue" in a way that helps you shift, not shut down. You need both. One reminds you that you are enough. The other pushes you to be better.

Be Patient. It's Not All Supposed to Happen Fast.

Most businesses do not hit in the first six months. Or even the first year.

And that is normal.

What is not helpful is measuring your success against someone else's timeline.

Or believing the myth that if it is not working fast, it is not meant to work.

Some things take time because they are worth building right. Give yourself permission to move slower, smarter, and with more intention.

This does not mean you stop pushing. It means you stop panicking.

Humor Is a Survival Skill

You will mess things up. You will pitch badly. You will send an email with the wrong link, forget a meeting, or blow a deadline.

You can either beat yourself up, or you can laugh, fix it, and keep moving.

A sense of humor does not make you less professional. It makes you more human.

And in business, being human is often what people remember most.

Before You Move On

Ask yourself:

- Where am I trying to figure it all out alone?
- What skills could I learn now to make better decisions later?
- Am I hiring or collaborating with people who fill real gaps?
- Who in my life grounds me emotionally?
- Who can I call for honest feedback?
- When was the last time I laughed at something that didn't go as planned?

This chapter is not about building your dream team overnight or collecting certificates. It is about not doing everything alone. It is about building enough support around you to go the distance.

Because once you've got the right people around you, it's time to ask a harder question. What does success look like for you, really? That's where we're headed next.

Chapter Ten

What Comes Next

Choosing Yourself and Moving Forward with Intention

This book has never been about turning you into something you are not. It has been about giving you space to ask whether this new direction, which is less structured and more self-led, is worth exploring.

Not everyone will choose to build a business. But everyone deserves the option to consider it. What comes next will not look the same for everyone. That is the point.

This Is Not About Labels

You do not need to call yourself an entrepreneur to build something meaningful. You do not have to work for yourself to take ownership of what is next. And you definitely do not need to swap one title for another to make your path valid.

This is about figuring out what feels right after a job ended, a role shifted, or a system pushed you out. It is about moving through loss, frustration, or uncertainty into something that fits better with who you are now.

Whether that becomes a business, a consulting path, a creative pursuit, or simply a more intentional career move, it matters. You are making choices. And that still counts.

The Work Is in the Trying

You cannot think your way into clarity. Eventually, you have to try something and see how it feels.

That might mean launching a simple service, putting together a basic offer, creating a budget, a calendar, or even just a few social posts. It could also mean attending a networking event in your area to start building new connections.

The point is not to get it perfect. It is to get it moving.

Trying shows you what works. Adjusting helps you get sharper. Repeating it turns motion into momentum.

You Are Allowed to Stay Small

There is no award for being constantly busy. There is no magic team size or revenue milestone that makes your decision legitimate.

You do not have to scale. You do not have to grow fast. You do not even have to turn your skills into a full-time business.

You just need clarity on what fits your life, your goals, and your capacity right now. If you decide to grow, let it be because you chose to, not because someone else's path made you feel like you should.

Letting Go Is Also Moving Forward

Maybe this idea helped you take a step. Maybe it gave you something to focus on while you navigate a big transition. And maybe, in the end, it is not something you want to keep building.

That does not mean it was a waste. Some ideas are bridges, not destinations. A path you choose not to take is still part of getting to the one that is right for you. Letting go is not quitting. Sometimes it is clarity.

You Still Get to Choose

What comes next is yours to define. You do not need a five-year plan. You do not need a perfect pitch or even a clear vision right now. But you do have the ability to make decisions with intention instead of reacting to circumstances.

You do not need permission to build what is next. You do not need to have all the answers. You just need to keep choosing yourself, quietly and consistently, in ways that add up.

You Are Not the Only One

There are people across every agency, office, lab, field crew, and department wondering the same thing. What else can I do with everything I know? How do I rebuild without a template? Where do I even start?

Some of them will never ask those questions out loud. But you did. That matters.

It means you are part of something, even if it is invisible right now.

Before You Close the Book

Ask yourself:

- What do I want more of in my work and in my life?

- What decisions have brought me closer to that?

- What am I ready to release?

- Who can I reach out to when I feel stuck or unsure?

- What is one small thing I can try this week to test a new direction?

You do not need certainty. You do not need speed. You just need to keep going.

You have done the thinking. You have asked better questions. What comes next is not about potential anymore. It is about what you actually choose to build.

There is no one right answer, but you are not doing this without support.

The next few pages include tools, prompts, and ways to connect if you are ready to take the next step.

After this Page

The Future Is Yours to Write

You've read enough advice. You've taken the time to think through the big questions. And hopefully, by now, you've started to see the outline of something new beginning to take shape.

You don't need to have every answer. But you do need to keep asking better questions. This isn't the end of anything. It's the part where you begin moving forward with more clarity, more self-respect, and a sharper understanding of what actually matters to you.

Whether you're already building something or still collecting tools for whatever comes next, it counts. This work matters.

So keep going. Ask for what you need. Try things. Change your mind. Start over if that's what it takes.

The future isn't fixed. It's built by people like you. People who show up, one decision at a time, and choose to keep moving.

You're more ready than you think.

Epilogue

The Door You Are Opening

This book was never intended to give you a definitive answer. It was meant to offer a place to begin.

You've explored what entrepreneurship could look like after a government career.

You've been given examples of where to start gathering information, finding community, and testing new possibilities. There's a resources section if you are ready to dig deeper into skills, services, or strategies that support your next steps.

But the most important tool you take with you is not a checklist or a template. It is discernment.

Discernment is not about hesitation, and it is not about waiting for certainty. It is about learning to pause long enough to figure out what makes sense for you. It means questioning the default path, recognizing what aligns with your values, and being willing to adjust when something no longer fits.

Moving forward with discernment means giving yourself permission to think critically, explore openly, and decide intentionally. Not because someone else told you what to do, but because you built your own understanding of what comes next.

You are not closing one chapter to rush into another. You are opening a door to a future you are allowed to shape on your terms.

Stay curious. Stay discerning. Stay open to what you might build next. And if you are looking for support, insight, or a place to start the conversation, you can find me at:

CuriousFutures.co, FoundHerForward.com, or on LinkedIn.

Appendix A

Entrepreneur Readiness Assessment

Is This a Business... or Just an Idea?

This isn't a personality quiz. There are no unicorns or hustle cult slogans here.

Just a few questions to help you figure out if entrepreneurship *right now* makes sense for you and what kind of entrepreneur you might be.

Part 1: Reality Check

Check the box that best matches your current state of mind and resources.

1. **I can name a real problem I want to solve.**

   ☐ Yes

   ☐ Sort of

   ☐ Not really

2. **I've thought about how this could generate revenue.**

   ☐ Yes

   ☐ In theory

   ☐ I'm hoping that part just works itself out

3. **I've talked to someone who would *actually* pay for what I'm offering.**

☐ Yes

☐ Not yet

☐ Just my friends and family

4. **I'm prepared to go without a steady paycheck for a while.**

☐ Yes

☐ For a limited time

☐ Absolutely not

5. **I have some time, energy, or resources I can commit to this.**

☐ Yes

☐ Barely

☐ Not sure what I'd even be committing to yet

Part 2: The Artist vs. Mechanic Spectrum

Entrepreneurs need both the creative spark *and* the operational muscle.

Where do you naturally lean?

Mark yourself on the line below:

Artist: Big vision, ideas flowing, loves storytelling, thrives in ambiguity

←——————————•——————————→

Mechanic: Precise, systems-driven, loves details, thrives in structure

Follow-up Question:

Can I partner, hire, or learn the skills from the side I lack?

☐ Yes

☐ Maybe

☐ That's the part that scares me

Part 3: Transferable Skills Inventory

Mark any that apply. These are your current skills, no degree required.

People/Creative Skills:

- Storytelling

- Customer insights

- Community building

- Sales

- Branding

- Public speaking

- Product ideas

Operational/Technical Skills:

- Budgeting

- Logistics

- Project management

- Regulatory/compliance

- Data analysis

- Process optimization

Technology Skills:

- Website or e-commerce setup

- UX/UI design or user research

- Coding (even basic HTML/CSS/SQL)

- Video production or editing

- Social media tools & automation

- CRM, analytics, or email platforms

- AI: ChatGPT, prompts, workflows, or automation tools

Leadership Skills:

- Decision-making under pressure

- Delegation

- Hiring

- Training

- Building partnerships

- Vision casting

- Managing uncertainty

Which 2–3 do you actually *enjoy* using?

Part 4: Your Gut Check

Rate each from 1 (not true at all) to 5 (absolutely true):

- I'm okay taking calculated risks without guaranteed outcomes.

- I can stay motivated without external validation.

- I'm resilient, setbacks don't completely take me out.

- I want to *build*, not just escape what I was doing.

- I believe I can learn what I don't yet know.

Final Prompt:

If I were to start something today, it would be

_____

because

_____

_____

What Your Answers Might Be Telling You

There's no scoring system here, just signals.

Look back at your responses and ask yourself:

You might be closer than you think if...

- You answered **"yes"** to at least 3 of the questions in Part 1.

- You know which side you lean toward in the **Artist vs. Mechanic** spectrum and you're open to filling in the gaps.

- You circled 2–3 **skills you genuinely enjoy** using.

- You rated yourself a 4 or 5 on most of the **Gut Check** prompts.

If that's you: Start mapping out your idea, test something small, or have a working session with someone who's done it before. You may just need a plan, not permission.

You're still circling the runway if...

- You're unclear on what problem you want to solve or how it might make money.

- You're not sure which of your skills are actually transferable.

- The thought of going without a steady paycheck made your chest tighten.

That's not a red flag, it's a *pause* point. Maybe this is the time to explore different models (freelance, part-time, advisory), build skills, or get clearer on your purpose before jumping into entrepreneurship.

Still interested? Choose your next step:

- **Reflect:** Revisit your answers in a few days. See what still resonates.

- **Research:** Look into business models that align with your skills and risk comfort.

- **Reconnect:** Book a short session with me to clarify your idea or talk through what's missing.

- **Refine:** Build business confidence and find your profitable path.

You don't have to have it all figured out. But if you want to move forward, start where you are.

Want a second set of eyes on your idea?

Book a short session | FoundHer Forward | Connect on LinkedIn

Appendix B

Resources

The following resources are intended to help you explore, learn, and connect as you navigate what comes next. Use what serves you. Leave what does not. Stay curious.

Social Media and Platforms to Explore

- **Substack** — independent writers, new media, newsletters

- **BlueSky** — decentralized social networking

- **Threads** — real-time conversations and updates

- **TikTok** — trend insights, idea testing, creative research

- **YouTube** — tutorials, thought leadership, skill-building content

Instagram Accounts to Follow:

- **The Female Founder Collective** — insights and support for women entrepreneurs

- **Foodboro** — community for food and beverage startup founders

- **The Economist** — global economics, policy, and innovation trends

Podcasts Worth Listening To

- **The Tomorrow Today Show** with Mike Lee — conversations about future trends

- **The Prof G Pod** with Scott Galloway — business, markets, and cultural commentary

- **This Woman Can** — career transitions and entrepreneurship for women over 40

- **MaYapinion** — diverse perspectives on leadership and personal growth

- **ReThinking** with Adam Grant — how to rethink assumptions and careers

Recommended Books

- **Abundance** by Ezra Klein and Derek Thompson — reimagining economics and the future

- **The Book of Alchemy** by Suleika Jaouad — personal transformation and creative resilience

- **We've Decided To Go In A Different Direction** by Tess Sanchez — navigating professional shifts with honesty and humor

Additional Resources

- **Kendra Losee's Camera Confidence Challenge** —
  academy.kendralosee.com/14-day-camera-confidence-challenge

  Build on-camera confidence to better present yourself and your business.

- **SCORE** — www.score.org

  Free small business mentoring, resources, and templates.

- **Online Learning Platforms**:

  - **LinkedIn Learning** — professional skill-building and certifications

  - **Khan Academy** — free education across a wide range of topics

  - **SHRM** (Society for Human Resource Management) — HR resources and professional development

Note:

These resources are starting points, not finish lines.

Use them to stay sharp, expand your network, and stay grounded in the fact that learning is part of the building process.

Acknowledgements

To Elizabeth Zamora for holding my innermost secrets and telling me to write this book. To Kendra Losee and Kyra Reed for our weekly meetings where we have encouraged and challenged each other to continually build businesses that help people. We always see what is possible even when it is not clear.

About the Author

Merril Gilbert is a strategist who sees what's coming and knows how to get there. With 25 years leading businesses across food, health, and consumer sectors, she has built a reputation for cutting through complexity and helping founders focus on what matters. As CEO of Curious Futures and creator of FoundHer Forward, Merril works with entrepreneurs navigating critical decisions, from scaling and raising capital to building resilient, market-ready operations. Known for her direct approach and future-facing insight, she helps people connect vision with execution and move forward with clarity and confidence.